The QUICK-FIX HANGOVER DETOX

99 WAYS TO FEEL 100 TIMES BETTER

Jane Scrivner

sourcebooks

Published by Sourcebooks, Inc.
P.O. Box 4410, Naperville, Illinois 60567-4410
(630) 961-3900
Fax: (630) 961-2168
www.sourcebooks.com

Originally published in 2001 by Piatkus Books, Great Britain

Library of Congress Cataloging-in-Publication Data:

Scrivner, Jane.
   The quick-fix hangover detox : 99 ways to feel 100 times better / by Jane Scrivner.
     p. cm.
   Includes bibliographical references and index.
   1.   Detoxification (Substance abuse treatment)--Popular works. 2.   Alcohol--Physiological effect--Popular works. 3.   Hangover cures--Popular works. I. Title.
   RC565.S365 2010
   362.29'18--dc22

                              2009049646

           Printed and bound in the United States of America.
             VP 10 9 8 7 6 5 4 3 2 1

CONTENTS

• • •

"WHAT'S YOUR POISON?"

• • •

The hangover is exactly that, the poisonous hangover from the night or day before due to the aftereffects of the alcoholic drinks on your body. Quite simply, you poison your body and it reacts badly—no surprise there. For those times when we have just too good a time and overdo it, here are some handy hints on ways to spend the day before, and the morning and the day after.

We know it's not good to get drunk and that it damages our bodies. We know that alcohol is addictive and a drug. We know how disgusting we feel the next day... but whatever we know and however much we know, if we drink alcohol, sooner or later we are going to drink too much!

We know we should stop when we feel "happy and relaxed" while drinking, but feeling happy and relaxed puts us in the mood for another drink—and so it goes on. After a drinking bout we feel ghastly and disgusting; our brain feels too big for our heads and our stomachs feel stewed.

Yet despite this we keep on going back for more, and the one lesson we just don't learn is that alcohol truly pickles the brain.

What can we do to avoid hangovers? This book contains countless suggestions for supplements, remedies, exercises, treatments, treats, and tellings-off. There are new attitudes, new ideas, and more effective solutions to get you through the overindulgence and apologize to your body for the overabuse. Prevention is better than cure, so we look at lots of ways to stop after-effects from being quite so terrible and prevent them from taking their toll in the first place.

Quite simply, detox your hangover and you need never say "never again."

The Quick-Fix Hangover Detox is arranged in three sections. Ideally you should read all three at a time when you are not even contemplating a drink—preparation and prevention is key.

BEFORE

Here are some essential preventative and preparatory steps to help you prepare for overindulgence, some key facts to arm yourself with for an evening or a day out involving alcohol, and some thoughts to consider just in case you were not entirely clear about how you might feel or what you will have actually done to your body by this time tomorrow.

If it is already tomorrow, don't punish yourself about what could have been. Go straight to "After."

If it is still "Before," then congratulations! Well done and read on.

DURING

Here we deal with how to cheat with alcohol, how not to drink too much, how not to drink at all, and how to put in place some sneaky steps to make tomorrow more bearable for everyone.

If you are just about to leave the house on a "big night out," then read this in the car or cab—there is still time to save the day.

AND AFTER

Shhhh! Very quietly now... "After" starts on page 41. Turn slowly to the section and see if you can focus on any of the suggestions on what to do, take, or think—no sudden moves now. Keep warm, drink lots of water, and take some advice.

HEALTH WARNING

• • •

Frequent reports have been written about the nutritional value of alcohol and its possible benefits in some cases, in regulated amounts. But whatever the findings, it is still a fact that alcohol in excess is damaging to your health, addictive, and destructive.

The only way to avoid a hangover is to not drink. Providing you with a "hangover detox" should in no way give the impression that you can drink to excess with no ill side effects from now on. On the contrary, excess drinking is bad for you, your body, and your long-term health. If you think you may have a problem, please seek professional advice immediately.

If any of the warning signs listed below apply to you, please consult your GP for help with controlling your alcoholic intake:

- You believe your drinking is damaging your health.

- You regularly drink more than the nationally recommended amounts.
- You feel you need to have a drink in order to function.
- You regularly drink alone to excess.
- You drink too much and lose judgment when drinking.

PART 1

BEFORE

Prevention is Better than Cure...

1 Trip down memory lane—some hangover facts

Hangovers affect people in many different ways, but some of the most common and familiar side effects of excessive drinking are headaches, nausea, dehydration, and tiredness.

- Headaches are mainly caused by dehydration—your brain becomes prunelike.
- Nausea is generally due to an empty acid stomach churning away (think green bile slopping about!).
- Dehydration occurs because alcohol is a diuretic—it actually encourages you to urinate and expel electrolytes that are needed for essential cell growth and repair, and your kidneys have to work overtime to process the excess fluids.
- And tiredness is due to the work your body is having to do to get better—not to mention the fact that you probably didn't get to bed before tomorrow and that when you did, your sleep was disturbed and fitful.

How could you do this to yourself?!

2 Water—the elixir of life

Dehydration is the main reason for feeling so awful after indulging. Alcohol is a diuretic—it actually encourages your body to lose fluids. So before, during, and after your "session" you absolutely must drink at least 1.5 liters or 3 pints of water a day. (You should be drinking this amount every day anyway.) This will help your body in two main ways:

- **Firstly**, it will completely hydrate your body in preparation for the huge fluid loss that excess drinking will cause.
- **Secondly**, it will help your body to flush through the alcohol and purge the poisons.

3 Get the munchies before you get the thirst

Don't drink on an empty stomach. Make sure that you eat something before you drink something.

Don't worry if there is a problem with healthy food being available—just get hold of anything edible. If you have an option, go for the more absorbent and bulky foods, such as breads, pastries, potatoes, and dips, rather than just grazing on nuts and chips.

If there are canapes available, choose sushi, bruschetta,

or potato skins rather than picking at olives and nuts, which are better for you but not substantial enough to help absorb the alcohol that is to follow or to line the stomach.

The nibbles provided with drinks are often dips or fried food that's high in salt to make you drink more, so beware, but just make sure you eat something. Drinking on a full stomach is much healthier and will probably mean you drink less.

Alcohol doesn't fill you up and isn't very nutritious—you just think it is after you have had a few.

4 Care for your kidneys

The kidneys process fluids. They will take on the bulk of the work during and after your "big night out." They also keep the PH (Positive Hydrogens—acid/alkaline) balance of your body in check, which helps to prevent the nauseous acid stomach that often comes as a result of overindulgence.

Alcohol is a diuretic, which means it will encourage your kidneys to process and pass much more fluid than actually goes in. Alcohol will also give you a very acidic stomach, which we all know leads to indigestion.

You need to drink loads of water and eat or drink anything that is good for the kidneys to keep them toned and ready for any action that lies ahead:

- **Black currant juice**—fresh, not concentrated!
- **Cranberry juice**—keeps the waterworks fresh and glowing
- **Celery and asparagus**—to make you pee efficiently
- **Bananas**—contain potassium to help process fluids

Include at least one of these in each meal in the run up to the fall-out.

5 Look out for your liver

The internal effects of your overindulgence are grim—alcohol poisons the system, and since the liver is the organ that processes the alcohol it therefore suffers the most damage. If you don't look after it and it gets overloaded it fights back and produces a toxin that will actually give you a headache.

Keep your liver cleansed, invigorated, and refreshed at all times and it will look after you in your darker moments on the drink. Take some tonics:

- **Beetroot juice or raw beetroot**—a liver tonic
- **Black grapes, big bunches**—high fluid content and antioxidant

- **Fresh garlic and garlic pills** (odorless ones are best)—cleansing and strengthening
- **Raw carrots or carrot juice**—tonic and cleansing
- **Fennel tea**—cleansing and flushing
- **Dandelion tea**—liver tonic and cleansing

These should all form part of your diet for the days preceding a big night out. Taking them regularly before taking your tipple could just let you get away with it totally—and if you can say that with no mistakes at the end of the evening you really are doing very well.

6 Stir-fry to sobriety

Fill your meals with antioxidant, protective, and strengthening foods. Chow down to drink up and feel the benefits of the added protection. All the foods in this recipe are strengthening, cleansing, or protective, or just packed full of antioxidants to make your recovery faster and more efficient.

STRENGTHENING STIR-FRY

2 tablespoons of olive oil
½ onion, finely diced
clove of garlic, thinly sliced
1 teaspoon of honey
1 tablespoon of sherry
1 tablespoon of Worcestershire sauce
2 or 3 broccoli florets, broken into small pieces
1 large carrot, thinly sliced
¼ of a small red cabbage, shredded
salmon steak grilled and flaked
short-grain brown rice, cooked and kept warm

Heat the oil in a heavy-bottomed pan or wok. Add the onion and garlic and fry until golden brown. Mix the honey, sherry, and Worcestershire sauce and put aside. Add the vegetables to the onions and garlic and fry until nicely browned. Add the salmon flakes, pour the juice mix over, and heat through, stirring occasionally. Remove from the heat and serve on the brown rice. Season to taste, although the sauce is quite tangy already.

Feel your body get ready for the fight.

7 Tea for you

Green tea is full of flavonoids, which are generally believed to be antioxidant, antibacterial, anti-inflammatory, and all-round health enhancers and improvers. The more you include in your diet, the more you are doing for your body. Drinking flavonoid-packed green tea is best. Green jasmine and oolong teas are very good, and then normal Indian, Earl Grey, and Ceylon black teas follow up the rear in terms of flavonoids. All these teas drunk in moderation will build your body's ability to defend itself when you declare hangover war. Decrease the caffeine and/or stimulant content by briefly steeping the tea in hot water. Throw away the first "brew" and then add more boiling water.

Drink one good cup of tea a day and protect yourself.

8 B pro-active...

It seems that vitamin B complex can save you from your worst hangover. It can decrease your flavor for alcohol, protect your body from pollutants or poisons, and protect your liver.

Take 100 mg of vitamin B before, during, and after your session and all will be well. You do need to repeat the dosage at these intervals as alcohol destroys the vitamin. If you forgot, or just got too drunk to remember, then take the same dosage the following day—morning (if you are up before midday), noon, and night.

Vitamin B15, if you can get hold of it from your local health store, is reputed to have the following properties:

- **It is water soluble**—good because you should be drinking a lot of water by now.
- **It can reduce your craving for alcohol**—so take it before you start drinking.
- **It can protect the liver against cirrhosis**—hopefully we have not got to this stage, but at least it should help your liver to a speedy recovery.

9 Live yogurt

"Arrests internal putrefaction, contains a natural antibiotic, and restores equilibrium."
—*Herbal Remedies and Home Comforts,* Jill Nice

Eat live yogurt in large amounts. Make sure you down as much as you can muster before embarking on your night out, as it will line and protect your stomach from the acidic onslaught. It is said to aid in recovery from diarrhea—no "running" to the loo! It also has a high content of lactobacillus acidophilus to regenerate intestinal flora that has been pickled from the proceedings.

If you make sure you eat plenty of yogurt before your session, you may just avoid the extreme circumstances described above.

10 The prickly protector

Milk thistle is a plant that can grow up to 6 feet high. Silymarin, a compound found in the seeds of this enormous plant, appears to be just fabulous for our livers.

Milk thistle strengthens and protects the liver, the very organ that is about to process all the alcoholic excess, so taking milk thistle before, during, and after your session will give you a "super liver," ready for anything you care to throw at it.

The liver eliminates toxins, reducing your body's toxicity. Having a super liver will help to:

- Cleanse the liver on a regular basis so that it can perform perfectly.
- Protect the liver from damaging effects of alcohol.
- Prevent the liver from overloading, thus reducing your hangover.

Take the recommended dosage of pills or tincture for 4 weeks prior to your period of indulgence. If you have indulged unexpectedly, then take emergency measures by having 1 teaspoon of tincture or 2 pills every 3 or 4 hours on the day after.

Note: Thank you to David and Frances for this one, which was tried for New Year 2000/2001 and passed admirably. One important hint though: it tastes disgusting so add honey or mix it with other teas.

11 Gym 'n' tonic

Getting fit will decrease the impact of your hangover. Pumping iron not only develops the muscles and skin tone but also works out your internal organs. Once they are working at peak efficiency, you will notice that the gap between damage and mending narrows. Your body will require less time to recover as everything will be working perfectly healthily—you will be firing on all cylinders and processing at top speed. As a result of working out regularly, your organs will be more efficient at working through the alcoholic toxins you care to throw at them.

Combining regular exercise and drinking healthy amounts of water to hydrate before, during, and after your session will build your body to the peak of perfection both outside and in.

Hone your body and halve your hangover.

12 Feed your liver

The following salad is a feast for your liver. Each ingredient is tonic, antioxidant, cleansing, or a digestive. It also happens to be quite delicious for any other occasion.

Have as much or as little as you want, but just don't leave any ingredients out!

crunchy red onion, sliced or diced
arugula leaves, loads of them
bags of baby spinach
squeeze of 1 whole lime
squeeze of 1 whole lemon
1 large or 2 small grated carrots
grated fresh ginger, to taste
sliced pickled or fresh beetroot
crushed garlic, amount depending on sociability!
olive oil, for drizzling freely
freshly ground or cracked peppercorns

Mix the whole lot in a huge bowl and tuck in with big chunks of brown whole-grain bread drizzled with olive oil and balsamic vinegar, or a large slice of grilled salmon placed on top.

13 Facts to put you off

Alcohol does many things to us and some of the most damaging can be listed as follows:

- It's expensive
- It's addictive
- It drains the body of essential nutrients
- It causes stomach problems
- It can lead to irritable bowel syndrome
- It can cause high blood pressure
- It may lead to malnutrition
- It can cause dry, pale skin

So, after your great night out, you can be left with any number of the above as well as a stinker of a headache and a stomach that feels like you've got several liters of olive oil swilling around inside it.

Maybe just one less next time?

14 Tears and tantrums

One of the big effects of alcohol—and there are many—is that it highlights emotional instability. If you are feeling a little bit wobbly on the emotional front, make sure you don't get wobbly on the alcohol front, too.

Unfortunately, the very time we think we need a drink—when we are upset or have had an argument, or when someone has been nasty to us—is the very time we should avoid a drink and keep a clear head.

Before embarking on a drinking session, check your motivation. Are you drinking to forget or to drown sorrows, or because you are hurt or upset? If the answer is "yes," stick to non-alcoholic drinks for now. You need to keep a clear head to enable you to sort things out. Save your drink for when you are feeling much more positive. Drink to celebrate or socialize, not to commiserate or hibernate.

So, no more tears: drink when you are happy and think when you are sad.

15 Detox to detox

If your body is cleansed within and there is nothing on the "to do" list for your internal organs, if you are fully hydrated and fighting fit, then your hangover will have a clear run through your body. Concentrate on cleansing your body and it will make light work of the job in hand.

Nothing gets in the way, everything is processed, and

you might just escape a hangover. Following a full detox program for ten to thirty days of healthy eating and exercise brings your body into tip-top health and fitness and balance. Detox regularly and you may give yourself an alcohol freebie.

16 **Know your limits**

Having a drink is great. Knowing your limit is even better and more helpful too. The weekly recommended maximum amounts of alcohol are:

14 units for women

21 units for men

These units should be taken during the course of the week, not all in one session. Binge drinking is the most harmful way to take alcohol—and make no mistake, our bodies let us know this.

Unfortunately, there is more bad news for women. Men have an enzyme that allows them to process alcohol more efficiently—so it is true, they can drink more than women without experiencing the same effects.

Some things in life are just not fair.

17 Ugly juice

Skin cells can only stay healthy, plump, and fresh if there is a good supply of water, which forms the bulk of the living cells in the body. Our skin also needs water for the cells to regenerate. Drinking alcohol regularly leads to dehydration of both the body and the skin.

Dehydrated skin looks dull, lined, tired, pale, and pasty.

Think fresh, plush, smooth, and velvety grape versus dried, old, knobbly prune.

18 Stop the ageing process

Drinking excess alcohol on a regular basis puts pressure on the facial blood vessels. Constant dilation of these vessels strains the elastin and collagen in the vessel wall, ultimately leading to collapse. This will show on your face.

Dehydration of the skin causes dryness and makes lines look more obvious and dark areas look darker as they sit more deeply on your face.

The life blood of our skin is water and alcohol drains the skin of water.

Put all these facts together and you can see that alcohol clearly accelerates the ageing process.

19 Fight the flab

Alcohol is fattening, so before embarking on an evening of tipples, think about a stomach with ripples—it's enough to drive you to drink! Here are some calculations:

Champagne	95 cals per 4 oz glass
Dry white wine	83 cals per 4 oz glass
Red wine	86 cals per 4 oz glass
Bottled lager	80 cals per 300 ml (½ pint)
Strong lager	165 cals per 300 ml (½ pint)
Cider	120 cals per 300 ml (½ pint)
Gin, vodka, whisky, and all major clear spirits	55 cals per 1 oz measure

The measures above are strict "pub" measures—nowhere near the amounts actually consumed when we pour our own drinks or leave it to our hosts to do so. Before you know it you could have had your 2,000/2,500 (female/male) daily recommended calorie quota without having touched real food, and then there's the munchies at the party, the homemade dip and chips, the macaroni and cheese at midnight...

20 Jumping juniper

Juniper is a diuretic. It tones the liver, keeps your waterworks healthy, and cleanses the skin. Juniper is positive and uplifting because it flushes out all the bad stuff in our bodies.

Try juniper tea, juniper supplements, or juniper essential oil in a rub, bath, or massage.

Take juniper and be positively raring to go!

21 Ginseng booster

Ginseng is a plant extract, an all-around healer and cure-all. It has the ability to bring the body back into balance, to rejuvenate, and to empower. It contains vitamins, minerals, and amino acids, and it balances blood sugar. Ginseng can be taken as a tea or supplement, or in honey as a tincture. It:

- Strengthens the liver
- Protects the liver
- Aids against toxic overload
- Removes internal stress
- Tones the liver
- Feeds vitamins, minerals, and amino acids to the body

- Maintains blood sugar levels
- Boosts the immune system

So boil the kettle and make a nice pot of ginseng tea, or take a regular supplement or a spoonful of tincture—all readily available from health food stores.

Gulp in the goodness.

22 Echinacea every day lets you work, rest, and play

Echinacea is a plant with a pretty little daisylike flower, but it's the properties of the root that can boost our immune systems. It builds the body's resistance to illness or speeds recovery if you become ill—or drunk. It is most commonly taken as a cold remedy or protector against colds and skin conditions.

Echinacea can be taken for prevention or for treatment. Prevention is always best! But afterward it's just as effective.

So, when you are burning the candle at both ends, pushing your body to its limits, and partying 'til you drop—you need to take some echinacea to return to fight another day.

23 Prepare for the morning after

Make sure your home is full of rescue remedies. In preparation for the morning after, you need to put some work in the day before.

Stock up on foods and beverages that repair, restore, strengthen, balance, cleanse, detox, flush, and make you feel good:

- Baked potato
- Brown rice
- Brown bread
- Carbonated water
- Fennel tea
- Fish
- Fresh fruits such as oranges, cranberries, bananas, pineapples, and black currants
- Fresh vegetables
- Honey
- Lemons
- Peppermint tea
- Raisins
- Sultanas
- Toasted oats or oatmeal
- Vitamins
- Yogurt

Make sure there is nothing to tempt you into old habits and everything to make you feel like new. Filling your house with foods that are easy to eat and very beneficial for recovery makes the hangover cure a no-brainer.

24 No vomiting—take Nux Vom

The homeopathic remedy Nux Vom, as well as being very appropriately named, is used to help addicts reject their alcohol cravings. Taking it may just reduce your intake and therefore your hangover.

Nux Vom helps to decrease the effect of your hangover by decreasing the damage the alcohol does to your body. It reduces headaches and nausea, so get some and follow the instructions to the letter.

Take Nux Vom before drinking and you may not drink as much. Carry on taking it the morning after until you feel 100 percent again.

Remember not to take peppermint or caffeine when taking homeopathic remedies—if you do they simply won't work.

25 Play consequences

Excess alcohol or even just a small amount will impair your judgment, reduce your inhibitions, and delay your response times and reflexes. You will feel braver than you should! We have all seen the pictures of the night before and stared at disbelief at the things we got up to...

When drinking you may do something or make a decision that you would never normally—soberly—dream of. Don't make a "drink decision" that you will regret for the rest of your life.

Don't:
- Drink and drive
- Leave a party with a total stranger
- Have sex with a stranger
- Start a fight
- Tell someone a secret that ought to stay secret

Do:
- Dance on the table
- Ask someone out on a date—at a later date
- Sing karaoke
- Do the Funky Chicken

Just have a good time without doing anything that may be used against you later!

26 Preparation is key

Before leaving for your night out, place the following by your bed:

- A large 2 liter (4 pint) bottle of water with a tumbler or glass
- A bowl or plate with slices of oranges and kiwi

...all will be revealed.

PART 2

DURING

Keep a Clear Head

27 Mother's ruin

When choosing your drink, think about these little known facts:

- It is common knowledge that gin is a depressant.
- It is less common knowledge that the quinine in tonic water is even more depressing.
- What is even more depressing than that is that alcohol is actually a depressant.

Depressing isn't it?

28 The feel-good factor

When we are drinking we reach a nice stage when we feel relaxed and happy. The biggest mistake we make is to believe that if we carry on drinking, we will become more relaxed and much more happy.

Stop drinking when you feel good, and stay that way.

29 Stop when you've had enough

Anyone who tries to force you to drink when you have said no to their offer is not a friend. Don't fall into the same trap.

Trying to get your friends to have just one more when they have declined your offer is stupid and irresponsible.

Make your offer and if they say no, offer a non-alcoholic alternative if you still want to buy them a drink. What does it matter to you what's in their glass?

Similarly, if you feel awkward about declining an offer of a drink, just request something non-alcoholic with a smile on your face. Your friends should be just as happy.

30 A sugar rush

Mixing sugar with alcohol—sweet spirits—speeds up the absorption of the alcohol. These drinks don't taste very alcoholic due to their high sugar content, so you could be on bottle three before bottle one kicks in.

You will simply get drunk, quicker.

The fresh, fruity color of these drinks gives them a promise of being healthy and exciting, but there is nothing healthy or exciting about the way you will feel after an evening on them. Steer clear of so-called alco pops, soft drinks, or fruit drinks premixed with alcohol, or caffeine-filled soft drinks mixed with alcohol. They look good but the next day you won't look anywhere near as colorful as they do.

31 Sweet high

Drinks with a high sugar content are deliberately designed to make you drink more. But the rush of energy you get from increasing your blood sugar and glucose levels will soon fall to way below where it was when you started your evening. You will reach for another drink just to keep your energy up.

These drinks should be reserved for the young—or young at heart—who have the energy to dance the night away, burn the sugar calories, and then remember to drink loads of water before crashing into bed.

Count me out...

32 Think before you drink

When ordering or accepting your next drink, just think:

- Alcohol rots your liver.
- It weakens your heart.
- It increases your risk of getting different cancers.
- It can lead to clinical depression.
- It may give you gout.
- It could promote osteoporosis.

You could sit this round out, and just have a good time and halve your hangover potential.

33 Hydrate to recuperate

Maintain your hydration levels by matching every alcoholic drink with the same amount of water. You can either dilute your drinks or make sure that every other drink is non-alcoholic. If you can find a way to make sure that your intake is not totally alcoholic you will greet the morning with a sunnier smile. Try the following:

- Drink water before leaving to go out for the evening.
- Order water with your wine or beer.
- Take alternate sips of water and alcoholic drink.
- Order a spritzer—soda mixed with your chosen alcohol.
- Accept a sparkling water with a slice of lime/lemon or orange.
- Drink a totally non-alcoholic drink and give your body time to absorb the alcohol already in your system.
- Drink slowly.
- Finish with water.

Finish on full hydration.

34 Fake it

If you feel awkward about not drinking or if you don't want people to know you are not drinking, then you can fake it. Bartenders, used to dealing with all matters alcoholic, are very good at not giving the game away. Remember:

- A sparkling water with ice and lemon in a spirit glass can look like a gin or vodka and tonic.
- Ask for low-alcohol or "light" beers or lagers in place of the full-strength variety. They all look exactly the same.
- Drink long drinks: have the alcohol but twice the amount of mixer, and add more mixer as you drink, not more alcohol.
- Replace gin or vodka with tonic water, rum with cola, whisky with ginger ale, vodka with cranberry juice, and tequila with lime juice.

No one needs to know.

35 Slow down and feel the effects...

It is likely that even when you think you've had enough, there is still enough alcohol in your system to have done quite enough damage and some that hasn't even had time to take effect.

If you are feeling good and mellow, order a soft drink or sit out the next round.

Wait for the alcohol in your system to take effect. If you are drinking very quickly you will gradually get more and more drunk without realizing that you have already achieved your goal. If you are drinking slowly, then feel the effects and don't waste any more hard-earned money.

36 Drinking *is* hard work

Think about how long you have to work to pay for your evening out.

Depending on where you live (or where you are drinking) the cost of your session can vary. Wherever you are—take a moment to think how long it took you to earn your drink.

A glass at lunch time, pre-dinner drinks, a bottle of wine with a meal, and one for the road could add up to a full day's work.

37 Keeping a balanced view

Our bodies are very clever, cleverer than most of us. They know when things are out of balance and they show the signs.

Lymph nodes limp due to and processing excess waste materials	Bags under eyes and tiredness
Skin a bit sad due to dehydration	Blotchy, spotty, congested skin that shows signs of cellulite
Kidneys not happy due to extra fluids in the body	Smelly, dark urine
Intestines imbalanced, too much acidity	Gas and wind
Liver not too hot, working hard, processing alcohol, and protecting you	Dog breath, camel, tongue, bloating, nausea, and indigestion

Drinking too much alcohol clearly unbalances your system.

38 Alcohol unbalances so much in fact that...

It makes you fall over and you:

- Rip your clothes
- Scuff your shoes
- Get muddy hands

- Lose your dignity
- Bloody your knees
- Have to explain to everyone why you have a black eye
- And basically don't look very attractive...

So balance your drinking and keep your balance.

39 The darker the brew, the more damaging to you

A common belief is that the color of your drink of choice denotes the damage it will do to your body. The darker the drink, the more damaging, goes the theory.

- Choose vodka, gin, white wine, or any other transparent and clear, clean, and fresh drink. It will leave you feeling just fine.
- Anything dark, mysterious, syrupy, and full of tannins will leave you with something to remember it by.

Try not to mix your drinks. Stick to just one type to allow your body to process the alcohol more efficiently. Working on several different alcohols and mixers is more arduous than working on lots of the same.

40 Flavonoids and polyphenols

Flavonoids and polyphenols are antioxidants. There are many types of flavonoids, and each foodstuff that contains flavonoids probably has around thirty or forty of them—so if it's got them, it's got a lot.

There is still lots of research to be done on flavonoids, but to date they are deemed to be incredibly good for you:

- Antioxidant
- Anti-inflammatory
- Antiviral
- Decrease the incidence of heart disease
- Decrease the incidence of strokes

Flavonoids can be found in black currants, bilberries (such as blueberries or huckleberries), cherries, red grapes, tea, apples, onions, and red wine.

So, do some research—order a full-bodied red and see if you feel any better the next day.

41 Drink your way to a healthy next day

You can actually aid your recovery process while you are drinking. Drinking fruit-based cocktails or drinks will ensure that you get all the vitamins, antioxidants, and alkalinity you need to recover while you are still drinking...

Cocktail	Benefits of ingredients
Honey Vodka	
Polish honey vodka	
Honey	accelerates expulsion of alcohol
Lemon juice	alkaline forming to protect your stomach
Angostura Bitters	natural, herbal digestive
Kiwi Daiquiri	
Havana Club	high vitamin C content
Fresh kiwi	
Sugar	
Cranberry Martini	
Cranberry vodka	high vitamin and fluid content
Fresh cranberries	protects against intestinal imbalance

Cocktail	Benefits of ingredients
Pineapple Breeze	
Pineapple vodka	protection, balance, vitamin C
Cranberry juice	helps digestion
Pineapple juice	
Zander Breezer	
Mount Gay Rum	
Midori	
Fresh mango	vitamin E, vitamin C, and antioxidant
Watermelon, blended	antioxidant
Kiwi, blended	vitamin C
Soda water	fluids, hydrating

Give it a try and see if the secret of the hangover cure is in the actual drinking. Proof of the pudding, so to speak.

Cocktails courtesy of Grant Collins, bar manager at Zander Bar, London

PART 3

AFTER

Never Again...

42 Put back what you get rid of

Before you left for your night out, you should have placed a bottle of water by your bed with some slices of fruit, yes? Good.

If you have been drinking, your sleep will be fitful and you will need to visit the bathroom on a regular basis.

Every time you go to the bathroom, take eight glugs of water and chomp three slices of fruit before climbing back into bed. Stay sitting up for the count of ten and then lie back down and try to sleep.

The water rehydrates your body each time you decrease essential fluid levels. The fruit pumps antioxidants for protection and vitamin C for recovery into your system at regular intervals. Sitting up for the count of ten will aid digestion and prevent reflux. Yuck.

43 Open the fridge door

First thing in the morning—or maybe not so "first thing"— you need to feed. Choosing a healthy breakfast may not be your first choice, but it truly is the quickest route to the road to recovery.

Reach for anything you have filled your fridge with in preparation—see page 44.

Yogurt	protective and balancing
Fresh fruits, such as oranges, cranberries, bananas, pineapple, black currants	full of vitamins, antioxidants, fluids, and nutrients
Toasted oats or oatmeal	absorbent and balancing
Lemons	alkaline forming
Honey	speeds up elimination of alcohol
Peppermint tea	digestive and settling
Fennel tea	cleansing
Fresh vegetables	antioxidant
Brown rice	absorbent and scouring, antacid
Brown bread	absorbent, roughage
Baked potato	absorbent and bulk
Fish	increase heart health
Vitamins	protective and nutritious
Sparkling water	oxygenating and hydrating

44 Don't go greasy

No matter how tempted you are to resort to a big, fried break-fast, just don't. Eat more muesli if you need to nibble, but don't go greasy. Just think of the grease, oil, and fats all churning up inside compared to the absorbent oats, nuts, and fruits.

Imagine how fried eggs and bacon would feel sliming around your stomach and through your body—a bit like a scene from a bad B movie. Big breakfasts filled with fried foods come with a label that says heavy, greasy, and sluggish.

- **Eggs**—not too bad—just don't fry them—poached or boiled is best
- **Bacon**—acid forming, stomach churning
- **Bread**—absorbent, whole wheat: OK
- **Sausages**—more acid to the mix and fatty, too
- **French fries**—fried, fattening, and greasy
- **Fried bread**—don't even go there
- **Hash browns**—potatoes, veggies, and a little oil—not too bad, but not great
- **Chocolates, pastries, muffins, cakes**—sugar high, then shocking low

45 Get minty fresh

Don't drink tea or coffee—your recovery brew should be herbal. Not only will it freshen the "day after" breath, but it will also almost certainly pep you up—that's why it's called peppermint!

Caffeine will simply increase your water loss due to its diuretic properties. Drink peppermint tea, rehydrate some more, and settle the bubbling digestion.

If you don't like the idea of peppermint tea, you can use peppermint essential oils in a rub or massage on your stomach. Mixed with a base oil or milk to disperse the oil, they will ease your digestive unrest.

It is no coincidence that anything medical for the stomach is minty flavored.

46 Get your oats

Oatmeal settles the stomach and decreases its acidity. It helps to stabilize blood sugar levels and absorb the toxins. Eat oatmeal for breakfast and eliminate the nausea often associated with alcoholic excess.

Serve it with grapefruit segments on top for cleansing and vitality. You can also stir in some honey or slice up a banana. Bananas lift your mood and give you a slow-release energy boost, so you should feel better sooner and for longer.

47 Honey, honey

Honey is set to become the elixir of life itself. The findings from each new study are revealing ever-increasing knowledge about the restorative properties of honey.

According to the National Headache Foundation, honey contains a sugar called fructose that actively competes for the body's normal metabolism of alcohol—thus speeding up the whole process of recovery.

A large mug of hot water and a teaspoon of honey in bed before you go to sleep is best. Start the process early if you can, but if this is not possible the morning after will be almost as good.

Honey also helps to balance the body, which means that there are no highs or lows as the body works on getting rid of the alcohol from the system. The more gradual the process, the less awful the headache.

48 Positive essentials

Take supplements of starflower or oil of evening primrose and see the world through rose-tinted spectacles.

Both oils contain GLA (gamma linolenic acid), which becomes Prostaglandin E1—a mood enhancer. Unfortunately, this enhancer can be destroyed by alcohol consumption.

Taking supplements will regulate your mood swings,

giving you energy that will help you to get through the darker hours.

49 A celery flush

Excess alcohol will make your stomach highly acidic, leading to nausea and upset.

Blend celery in a blender and drink the juice; alternatively, simply crunch on a celery stick. The alkaline in celery will balance the acidity of your current stomach contents—if you still have them.

Simple, yet effective.

50 Get a grip on your headache

One of the worst effects of a hangover is the headache. Feeling like someone has placed a vice around your head and is slowly tightening it leads to sensations of nausea, blindness, and pure misery.

Invest in some rosemary, peppermint, and lavender essential oils, and put one drop of each on a flannel or tea towel. Wrap this around a bag of frozen peas and place on your forehead as you recline. Leave on your head for 1 minute and then remove. Replace every few moments until the grip of your headache loosens and the pain subsides.

Now refreeze the bag of peas in readiness for your next celebration!

51 **A bitter pill**

Taking Caladium, a homeopathic remedy derived from an American arum plant, fifteen minutes before or after food on the day of your mighty hangover should help to prevent the extreme circumstances you may have put yourself in. Take Caladium before or after each meal and end the day in one piece.

52 **Orange zinger**

Blend together:
juice and pulp of 3 carrots
juice of 1 lime
juice of 1 lemon
a little grated fresh ginger
a spoonful of honey

- Carrot is an antioxidant and improves digestion.
- Lemon and lime balance acidity.
- Ginger is good for an unhappy digestive system.
- Honey will metabolize alcohol and keep your blood sugar up.

53 Lemon aid

- Counters and reduces acidity
- Alkaline forming
- Aids digestion
- Promotes circulation
- Protects and cleanses the liver

To make some fresh, homemade lemonade, quite simply combine:

3 lemons
1.2 liters (2 pints) water
2 oz sugar

Peel the rind off the lemons, then put the rind, water, and sugar into a pan and bring to the boil. Stir until all the sugar has dissolved, then simmer for 5 minutes. Allow to cool, and then squeeze the juice of the lemons and mix into the blend. Serve chilled or at room temperature.

54 Hot toddy for the poor body

A bedtime comforter, this one is good before you go to bed, but if you didn't quite manage it then, now is the time. Combine: hot water, lemon, and a few slices of fresh ginger.

- The ginger neutralizes acids in the stomach.
- The honey is healing.
- The lemon is alkaline forming.

55 Ginger drops

Ginger is wonderfully soothing, since it has both digestive and sedative properties.

- Place some ginger essential oil in a burner to ease the air.
- Add some fresh, grated ginger root to your salad to help settle the stomach.
- Drop some essential oil in your bath and wash away the blues—dilute the oil first in sunflower oil or milk to disperse it.
- Or simply drop some oil on a handkerchief and inhale nice and slowly.

56 Charcoal biscuits

An antidote for acidity, charcoal biscuits help to prevent wind, heartburn, and nausea—pass the packet now! Or take the pills for a more concentrated form of charcoal.

Don't try the stuff sold for use on barbecues—it's just not refined enough!

57 Slippery character

Slippery elm is great for combating the after-effects of your alcoholic haze. Its properties are believed to reduce acid indigestion and to prevent diarrhea. It is taken either as a supplement or as the powdered bark.

Make a nice tea, tuck up, and tuck in:

Mix some slippery elm powder to a paste. Add hot water while stirring until the mug or cup is full. For extra flavor, use a cinnamon stick to stir in honey to sweeten and/or nutmeg to taste.

If you have your wits about you or your drinking session took place during the day, you can use hot milk instead of water to make a comforting bedtime drink and let the slumber hours do the repairs.

If this idea sounds just too slimy, you can take your slippery elm in pill or tincture form. Remember, the worse it tastes the better it will be for you!

58 Flatulence no more...

The following will prevent any unfortunate and untimely "perfumed puffs":

- **Homemade lemonade** (see page 50)—drink freely to reduce acidity
- **Lemon barley water**—drink freely to aid digestion
- **Oatmeal** (see page 46)—breakfast fortification to balance blood sugar and acidity
- **Goat's milk or yogurt**—make your oatmeal with this to ease flatulence
- **Cloves**—add to hot water for a clove tisane, which will reduce gas and act as pain relief
- **Cinnamon**—sprinkle a little on your goat's milk oatmeal to reduce gas production
- **Peppermint** (see page 68)—try tea for your morning makeover as an aid to digestion

59 Dog breath

Waking up with your mouth feeling like cardboard and smelling as sweet as a camel's armpit—if they have armpits—is destined to have you spending much of the day at home alone.

Yogurt to the rescue: take one bowl of the stuff, natural and live, and it will not only cure your hangover but also banish the bad breath. The enzymes in yogurt neutralize nasty niffs.

It's quite amazing how something so plain can be so useful.

60 Bubbling back to sparkling health

Too much fizz the night before has done the harm, so try a little fizz the morning after—not the alcoholic kind, but carbonated water this time. Drink a little and feel the bubbles reoxygenate your blood.

Oxygenated blood relaxes the body and allows it to get on with the recovery process.

61 Pure gas

If drinking bubbles is not enough, then you can always go for the real thing.

Pure oxygen (see page 93) will drift you back to reality. Truly oxygenate your blood and feed your body. Normal air contains 26 percent oxygen. Taking oxygen from a flask or mask will pump up to 80 percent of the pure stuff into your system.

- Visit a trendy oxygen bar.
- Buy a canister of peppermint-flavored gas.
- Book into a spa with an oxygen room or treatment, and breathe yourself better.

In reality, most of us cannot do this, so why not wrap up and step out. Take a slow walk in the country or along the seashore, visit a park, or just sit in the garden for a while. Breathe slowly and deeply and feel the cells plump back to life.

62 Couch potato

A hangover puts strain on your body, especially on your heart, liver, and brain. It is even possible to suffer cardiac and other problems while exercising with a hangover.

Even without exercise, you are already pumping every

drop of fluid out of your body due to the excess diuretic in your system. Your kidneys are working very hard and passing more water than is taken in. A workout involving heavy sweating causes further water and electrolyte loss—both all-important to normal cell survival and function.

You have full permission to do absolutely nothing—slob out, throw a sicky, do nada, veg, or just play zombie.

Stay in bed, or if you are feeling very energetic, read a book or operate the remote control—slowly now.

63 All-day breakfast

Hangovers are for snackers. They're a pink ticket to graze all day. Too much food will make you feel sick and too little will make you feel sleepy. Nibble all day—five small meals will help to keep your blood sugar level, and drinking water every hour will make fluid levels manageable and snoozing will give your body time to recover.

Whatever you choose to eat or drink, make sure it is healthy and often. Eat plenty of fresh vegetables, fruits, salads, brown rice, grilled fish or white meat, seeds, nuts, and pulses. You can graze on these throughout the day as you need to keep your metabolism steady and your processing constant.

Get the toxins out and the life back in.

64 Don't glow too far

If you really feel you need to get out, take it easy. Do exactly what you want to do but take it slowly.

Exercise is good for your current state but don't overdo it. Don't put excess pressure on your body when it is already working hard to get back to balance.

Go out for a gentle, slow stroll to increase your circulation just a little. Do some mild activity to purge the toxins: tidy up your home—especially if your hangover is a result of having people at home—but don't work too hard. Do just enough to give you a bit of a glow.

Once the blood is flowing freely you can sit back, put your feet up, and recover in peace.

65 Herbal bed

If you have survived the day, you should have a relaxing lavender bath before you go to bed and get an early night. Bathing in lavender will ease dehydration and muscle tension, encourage cell growth, balance your mood, and relax you in preparation for a much-needed night's sleep. Lavender will calm, soothe, and balance you.

So run the bath, close the windows, let the room steam up, and sprinkle your lavender blend over the surface of the water. Slide gently into the bath and inhale the aroma with steady, deep breaths. Support your head with a bath pillow if you want to be really indulgent, soak away your nausea and feel the last evidence of the night before disappear into the atmosphere.

Note: To use pure essential oils in water you need to mix 5 drops of your chosen essential oil in a tablespoon of sunflower oil, milk, or pure alcohol (vodka is OK) to break it down and help it to disperse.

66 Mango and melon smoothie

Take one fresh mango and one melon—use honeydew or cantaloupe melon, but not watermelon, which is too watery, as its name suggests.

If you have a juicer—great; if not, just slice the mango and melon and drop the slices into a blender. Blend until smooth, and if you need more fluid, add a little apple juice and/or water.

Mango is full of beta carotene and vitamin B3, while melons are full of vitamins B1, B2, B6, and beta carotene. Both fruits are cleansers and encourage speedy digestion—excellent when trying to come back from a hangover.

67 Meditate to alleviate

Concentrating on yourself will give your body time to sort itself out and rebuild. It will make you feel calm, cool, and collected and stop the internal fever that is brewing.

Sit or lie comfortably in a warm room, with your back supported and neck relaxed. Place your palms facing upward, resting either on your thighs or on the floor by your sides. Take really deep, slow breaths in through your nose (this moistens and cleanses the air). Hold your breath for the count of four, then open your mouth and let the air flow out for the count of eight. Let all thoughts of the night before pass through your mind and do not dwell on any of them—just pass them through.

Picture your internal organs and systems one by one. See them working and pumping, and then see them healthy and fresh. Move from one part of the body to the next, seeing it work and then relax. Just let the thoughts drift through your head until all areas of imbalance have been seen as working and healthy again.

When all is well with mind and body it is time for you to return to the real world—take a deep breath and slowly open your eyes. You will feel refreshed and recovered. Thank you, body!

68 Cool as a cucumber

If you have the energy—possibly later in the day—you can try some rejuvenating treatments.

You will need:
a cucumber
peppermint essential oil
a hand towel

Slice the cucumber into really thin slivers. Fill a bowl full of very warm water and add 4 drops of peppermint essential oil.

Take the hand towel and soak in the peppermint water. Wring out the towel so that the water doesn't drip but the towel is still hot and minty.

Roll the towel into a bolster and lie back on a bed or couch. Place the bolster under the back of your neck so that it feels comfortable and supportive. Place the slices of cucumber over each eye and all over the face and neck.

Lie back, take some deep breaths, and let the warm peppermint sink into your body and soothe your muscles while the cooling cucumber takes away the puffiness and nourishes your ravaged skin.

69 Moisture booster

Your skin has taken a hit from both inside and outside. This delicious balm will bring it back to life, plump and refreshed.

You'll have moisturized skin in moments.

You will need:
honey—preferably one that is organic and natural, containing eucalyptus or some other floral extract juice of a lime flannel or piece of cotton sheets or pillow case
thin cucumber slices
grapefruit essential oil

Mix a tablespoon of honey with the lime juice—add it drop by drop until you have a thinner, paint-like consistency.

Place the flannel in some ice-cold water, then squeeze out all the water, roll the flannel, and place in the fridge for a few moments. Slice the cucumber. Remove the flannel from the fridge and drop some grapefruit essential oil onto one side.

Using a mirror and your fingers or a paintbrush, cover your face with a thin film of the honey and lime blend. Leave a circle around the eye area but take the blend onto your neck.

Lie down in a comfortable, warm spot and place the ice-cool compress oil drops upward on to your forehead. Place the cucumber slices over each eye. Leave for 15 minutes, then rinse thoroughly with warm water and pat dry.

70 Foot fun

If you have a foot bath—wonderful. If you are like me, a washing-up bowl will do the job—it's not as exotic but it does the same thing. This blend of oils is designed to totally revive a hungover body. Applied to the feet and reflex points, it reaches every part of mind, body, and soul.

You should feel refreshed, rejuvenated, rubbed, and totally revived.

Gather together:
2 bowls (both feet should fit inside each one), filled with

warm and ice-cold water
rose, lemon, peppermint, and pine essential oils
goat's, sheep's, rice, or cow's milk
some rose petals—or petals from any flowers from your
garden or any arrangements you happen to have around
the house. Just a handful will do; don't destroy the display
or make your garden bare.

Fill one bowl with enough water warm to put your feet in. Put 4 drops of rose essential oil and 2 drops each of lemon, peppermint, and pine essential oils into a tablespoon of milk. Pour into the bowl of water. Make up the same blend again and drop into a small bowl of oil for later use as your massage blend.

Sprinkle the petals onto the surface of the water. Fill the other bowl with very cold water.

Place your feet in the warm floral bowl and relax for 5 minutes. Place your feet in the cold water for just 1 minute. Put your feet back into the warm water for another 5 minutes and then remove and pat dry.

While your feet are still warm, rub them gently with your thumbs and fingers and remove any dry skin from between the toes, over the ankles, and by the ankle bones. Rub the soles of your feet and remove any dry skin from them.

Using the massage blend, massage your feet, working every area in both short and long strokes. Don't forget the area between the toes. Wrap your feet in a warm towel and lie back.

71 Detox bathing

Fill a bath, add some essential oils, and let your body purge the toxins.

Mix together:

2 drops ginger for antacid

2 drops rosemary for cleansing

2 drops grapefruit for stimulation

2 drops mandarin to boost your brain cells

2 tablespoons sunflower oil, vodka, or milk to disperse

Run a bath, sprinkle the blend across the surface and slip into the water. Wait for the poisons to float away. Take some really deep breaths down into your belly and try to relax.

When leaving the bath, pat your skin dry so that any residual oils are left to seep into your skin.

Wrap up warm and go back to bed.

72 The great eliminator

There are reflex points around the body that relate to the entire body. One of them, called the great eliminator, is situated between the thumb and forefinger.

Using the thumb and forefinger of your left hand, squeeze the triangle of flesh between the thumb and forefinger of the right hand. Go slowly and squeeze gently at first—if you have a hangover, this will be painful. Hold the squeeze for a few moments and then release. Repeat until the pain subsides, then swap over to the other hand.

Squeeze out the pain...

73 Just don't

The temptation to reach for the pills or chemical stimulants when you awake with your bad body is strong—but don't do it. You feel bad for a reason: you poisoned yourself. Feel the symptoms and treat them.

- Painkillers are acid-forming and will make your stomach feel grotty.
- Caffeine will give you a momentary high from which you will topple even further.
- And any other form of stimulant or drug is quite simply damaging—if not illegal.

Don't bribe or cheat your body; make sure your recovery is natural and nutritious.

74 Recover in the privacy of your own home

Your intestines are churning and the alcohol-induced change in environment is likely to cause gaseous exchange and softer stools.

I think you know what I'm saying.

75 Sweet smell of success

A good way to keep stools solid is to rub a blend of geranium and ginger over your lower abdomen.

Mix 2 drops each of these essential oils in 1 tablespoon of olive, grape-seed, or almond oil. Work the blend clockwise in circles around your stomach area. The oils will correct any imbalance and stop any short-notice calls to the bathroom.

76 Crystal ball

Crystals hold many, many healing properties. Sort through your jewelry box (or your lady friend's jewelry box) and see if there is anything there to bring back your sparkle.

Crystal	Good for
Amethysts	headaches
	detoxifying
	dehydration
	acid indigestion
Turquoise	addiction
	diarrhea
	sobriety
Rhodonite	first aid
	rescue
	sobriety

Crystal	Good for
Actinolite	liver
	kidneys
	detoxifying
Tourmeline	liver
	kidneys
Green Opals	kidneys
	detoxifying
Emeralds	headaches
	detoxifying

77 Positive potion

Peppermint essential oil could just be your life-saver. It:

- Sorts out your rumbling digestion
- Wakes up your stomach
- Wakes up your liver
- Is antispasmodic—stops the gripes
- Cleanses the skin
- Relieves the headaches
- Clears the head
- Relieves your nausea

In the morning, rub a few drops of peppermint oil mixed

into a massage oil—sunflower oil or grape-seed oil or even vegetable oil if you are in real trouble—onto your temples and tummy.

Drop a few splashes of oil into a bowl of hot water, cover your head and the bowl with a towel, and inhale your way back to the land of the living.

Alternatively, if these suggestions are far too energetic, drop 5 drops of oil onto a folded handkerchief, lie back, and inhale slowly.

Minty fresh once again!

78 **The show must go on**

We've all done it: just when we need to be in tip-top condition, acutely alert, chatty and charming, intelligent and punchy, cool and cute, we blow it all by going out and getting trashed the night before the big day. Bottle the following blend of essential oils and have them stored on standby in a cool, dark place—just where you should be right now!

- **5 drops grapefruit**—refreshing and cleansing
- **4 drops rosemary**—balancing and strengthens the liver
- **2 drops each juniper and fennel**—detoxing in every way

- Bathe in it.
- Shower using drops of the blend on your flannel.
- Mix with water and spray into a room.
- Burn it in a burner.
- Inhale it from a bowl.
- Mix in with a tablespoon of carrier oil and rub over back of neck and kidney area.
- Drop 1 drop onto a lightbulb that is switched on.
- Dribble a little on a radiator that is turned on as well.
- Book a massage and take your rescue blend with you.

Make it through your meeting and collapse into slumber on the other side.

79 Another liver tonic

Essential oils are extremely effective at working on the internal organs without having to undertake major surgery! Ideally, after a heavy session you would want to take out your liver, run it under some refreshing water, and put it back refreshed and revived. Essential oils can do this for you.

Put 2 drops each of lavender, frankincense, rose, and calendula essential oils in a tablespoon of almond or grape-seed oil and gently massage into the stomach and ribcage area.

These oils will do the liver cleanse from outside as well as inside.

80 **No-brainer**

Ok, so you have the hangover from hell? Just eat what it says on the following pages, at the times it says to eat. When you are not eating, you should be resting. When the day is over, go to bed. Don't do anything else and all will be well, I promise.

Breakfast—on rising—could be morning, could be afternoon:
Large mug of peppermint tea. And another one.
Large bowl of natural yogurt. Add a handful of nuts and muesli and chop in a banana. Eat slowly.

Half an hour later:
Large glass of water.

Snack 2 hours after breakfast:
Mango and Melon Smoothie (see page 58).

Lunch—2 hours after snack:
Brown rice, sliced beetroot, and grated carrot with a tin of tuna emptied over the top. Drizzle in some olive oil, and squeeze in a whole lemon. Mix together and tuck in. Chew slowly and stop to breathe once in a while.

Half an hour later:
Large mug of chamomile tea.

Snack—2 hours after lunch:
An apple, orange, and banana, chopped up, mixed with a teaspoon of honey and a dollop of yogurt.

Supper—3 hours after snack:
Grilled salmon steak with grated ginger, baked potato, and grilled red peppers.

Before bed or in bed before snoozing:
Hot toddy: boiling water in a mug, with 1 teaspoon of honey, a slice of ginger, and a squeeze of lemon juice.

Lights out and off to Bedfordshire. Zzzzzzzzzzz

81 Chakra balancing

You may already have heard of chakras; what is almost certain is that yours are currently out of balance. Chakras are spinning vortices of energy within our bodies that are based in ancient Indian healing. The word "chakra" comes from the Indian word "Sanskrit," meaning "wheel." When these spinning energy centers are all working together, we are in balance and feel good; when we throw them out—perhaps due to too much alcohol—we don't feel quite so well.

The main chakras that are affected by overindulgence are the root chakra, relating to the liver, kidneys, and metabolism and found between the legs and the solar plexus, relating to the adrenal glands and blood sugar levels, found just under the breast bone.

To get the chakras back into balance, lie down in a comfortable spot, place one hand on the groin area and the other on the solar plexus, and visualize the wheels spinning in a controlled and balanced rhythm. Concentrate on the flow and see if you can bring your energy back into balance.

82 Afternoon delight

Getting personal with your partner is a natural way to make a quick recovery. Making love releases the feel-good factor endorphins into the body. These endorphins also carry a natural analgesic—or painkillers to you and me.

Bednastics will increase circulation—blood flow to all areas of your body. Deep breathing will help to oxygenate your blood. Blood will drain from your throbbing brain—reducing your headache. Post-coital snoozing will relax and refresh you.

Practice safely now...

83 Banana bounce back

This method is tried and tested and was suggested by more than one "researchee," and all for good reason, it seems.

Slow-release sugars in bananas fill you up and their sweetness softens the blow and relieves the diarrhea; sugars stimulate serotonin to raise your mood, while potassium balances the fluids and regulates blood pressure. Your energy is raised. Honey expels the alcohol, and milk, cream, or yogurt says sorry to your stomach. Chuck it all in a blender and suck soothingly through a straw.

Soothe yourself with your smoothie.
 1 or 2 bananas, to taste
 1 teaspoon runny honey—dip your spoon in boiling water
 and the honey will slip off with no problem
 1 tablespoon cream grated nutmeg

Blend together, then add milk little by little to get the consistency you require. (For a low-fat version you can use yogurt in place of cream.) Sprinkle with nutmeg.

84 Say NO to caffeine

Reaching for a black coffee is just about the worst setback you can give yourself. The black, treacly gunk will set you back days from your road to recovery.

- It's a diuretic and will make you get rid of any fluids your body is trying to hang on to.
- It will give you a momentary rise in energy only to make you plummet even further into the depths of hangover hell.
- It will prevent absorption of any vitamins you have managed to eat at best, and at worst will kill them off completely.

Stay clear of coffee, sugar drinks with caffeine, colas, and stimulating fizzy drinks.

Just say no!

85 Say NO to drugs

The belief that taking aspirin can thin the blood and make the alcohol exit your body quicker is an old wives' tale. If anything, it will make your hangover worse, as it will increase the ratio of blood to alcohol in your body. You get drunk quicker and the effects are more horrible.

Taking painkillers the day after or even at your bedside before slumber is not going to do you any good, either. Many painkillers are actually acidic and act as irritants to your stomach lining—it is already pretty cross with you for putting the alcohol in, so don't make matters worse!

So, drink the water—just don't swallow the pill. If you absolutely must take something, make sure it is water-soluble and take it with food—never on an empty stomach.

86 Repair job

Alcohol does all sorts of damage, so make sure you do all sorts of repairs. Antioxidants are substances found in foods that boost the body's defenses. They reduce tissue damage and limit the growth of damaging cells. Without antioxidants, free radicals can cause undue and harmful effects on our bodies. Sounds awful.

Include as many antioxidant foods in your hangover

cures as possible, especially in the next 12 hours. Choose from the list below and tuck in. Raw foods are best, and slightly cooked foods are good.

Red peppers, satsumas, sweet potatoes, broccoli, carrots, cabbage (red and green), lettuce and other greens, bilberrys (such as blueberries or huckleberries), oranges, tea, sunflower oils and seeds, brussels sprouts, cauliflower, pumpkins, squashes, spinach, tomato, watercress, apples, apricots, black currants, parsley, wheat germ, liver, eggs, avocados, chicken, kidneys, sardines, mackerel.

87 The antioxidant potion

The following juice should be taken after a session.

Liquidize:

- **1 whole romaine lettuce**—Contains antioxidants, vitamin C, iron, digestive properties, and a powerful liver tonic.
- **1 large floret of broccoli**—Contains antioxidants, vitamin C, vitamin B, and iron and is rich in minerals.
- **Large handful of rinsed spinach**—Contains antioxidants, vitamin C and E, and iron.

Beef up your body's ability to fight back and race to recovery.

88 The Venezuelan way

The Venezuelan Air Force has clearly found a need to recover from times of rare overindulgence! A tablespoon of olive oil before the session and a whole guava fruit afterward. The theory is that olive oil will protect the stomach from the alcohol and the guava is packed full of vitamin C. And both are readily available on their tours of duty.

89 Peruvian potions

Travel to Peru and overindulge and you will be prescribed cat's claw tea or mate de coca tea or leaves—all available in pill or tea form from your local health-food shop. Both are reputed to cleanse and purify at the same time as settling an upset stomach or nausea. Cure yourself the Inca way.

90 A Dutch dare

Slipping a whole soused herring down your hungover throat is reported to do the trick...and if it doesn't there won't be anything left inside your body to cause you any further disruption or discomfort.

You may remove the head and eyes if preferred.

Thank you to Rob for this one—I think?!

91 Antipodean answer

Known for their ability to imbibe, the Aussies have a snack designed to do the trick.

2 or 3 tomatoes, chopped
a little chilli, deseeded and chopped
6 eggs
seasoning
a little milk and yogurt
olive oil
small slice of butter
sliced avocado—nice and fresh

Whisk the eggs, season, and add some milk and a little yogurt. Heat some olive oil and the butter in a large frying pan. Pour in the egg blend and cook lightly. Add the tomato and chilli and fold into the omelet.

When the omelet is cooked through—you can toss it if you are feeling adventurous, or grill the top to a nice, brown tan. Serve with the fresh slices of avocado.

All the nutrients to bring you back from down under. G'day mate!

PART 4

HAIR OF THE DOG

92 Buck's fizz—start as you mean to go on

Start the evening with champagne and orange juice.

Combine a quarter OJ with three-quarters champagne.

Add a dash of grenadine and a squeeze of lime juice... and continue the morning after. Just remember to stop at one glass!

93 Boost your energy

Two cocktails to get you started. Choose the one you fancy and watch it work.

BOOST
2 oz vodka
juice of half a carrot
juice of half an orange
juice of an apple
fresh ginger and ginseng

Mix the magic.

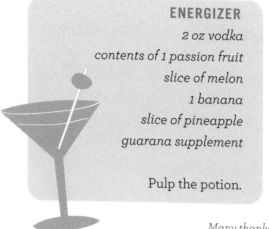

ENERGIZER

2 oz vodka
contents of 1 passion fruit
slice of melon
1 banana
slice of pineapple
guarana supplement

Pulp the potion.

Many thanks to Grant Collins,
bar manager at Zander Bar,
London.

94 Prairie oyster Cajun style

2 oz vodka
2 dashes Tabasco
cracked black peppercorns
serve in a glass dipped in celery salt
garnish with a fresh oyster

Down that and the hangover will tipple into insignificance.

Many thanks to Grant Collins, bar manager at Zander Bar, London.

95 Bloody Mary

juice ½ lemon
splash Tabasco, to taste
splash Worcestershire sauce, to taste
single (2 oz) or double (4 oz) vodka
tomato juice, fresh or carton
long stick celery
sea salt or celery salt
freshly ground pepper
lots of cooling ice

Mix the first four ingredients together, add tomato juice to the strength you like and season. Stir the whole lot with the celery stick and feed your hangover.

Rumor has it that a "bloodshot" is the same as the above, but substitute 2 oz condensed chicken or beef consomme for the tomato and exchange the celery stick for a long slice of cucumber. Interesting and well worth a go.

96 Irish Jig

Try a Black Velvet.

This is half Guinness and half champagne. Pour the Guinness (or stout) slowly, pour the champagne even slower, and drink slowly.

Iron, fizz, and a little luxury.

PART 5

IF YOU CAN'T BEAT THEM, JOIN THEM

97 Roll in it, bathe in it, and drink it

What a wonderful way to go! Sample some vinotherapie.

The owners of Les Sources de Caudalie in France discovered that the polyphenols in grape seed could be extracted and made into a full and exotic skin care range.

Polyphenol is an antioxidant and is hugely regenerative and restorative—just what you need. So, whether you drink it, wear it, rub it in, bathe in it, roll in it, or get all wrapped up in it—wine can be good for you! Reputed to be far better at combating the signs of ageing, the effects of pollution, and the damage caused by smoking, there can be no better place to overindulge and recover without leaving the building.

You can take a:

· Red vine bath
· Barrel bath
· Wine and honey wrap
· Merlot wrap
· Sauvignon massage
· Vrilles de vigne lymphatic drainage
· Crushed cabernet body scrub
· Anti-ageing vino lift
· Premier grand cru skin treatment

You can also:
- Infuse in a hot tub with grape seed extract.
- Be painted in wine and Bordeaux honey and left to slow cook.
- Drink in the amazing views of the French countryside.
- Walk in the surrounding vineyards.
- Sample the red vine tisanes and guzzle the grape juice, and when you have just about had it all you can sit down to a gastronomic feast without busting the waistline.
- You can find me in the hot tub next to yours.

98 Reason for celebration?

Madame Bollinger is famously reputed to have made the following reply when asked about her champagne drinking habits:

I drink it when I am happy and when I am sad. Sometimes I drink it when I'm alone. When I have company I consider it obligatory. I trifle with it if I'm not hungry and drink it when I am. Otherwise I never touch it—unless I am thirsty.

Sometimes it is good to take a lead from someone who knows their subject.

99 Dr. Bach's rescue remedy

Bach Flower Remedies are natural flower essences preserved in brandy no less. The Rescue Remedy contains the most commonly used remedies together in one bottle.

- Star of Bethlehem for shock
- Rock rose for great fear and panic
- Impatiens for mental and physical tension, when the sufferer cannot relax and the mind is agitated and irritable
- Cherry plum for loss of emotional control, screaming, shouting, and hysterical behavior
- Clematis for the bemused, the distant, and those feeling faint

Place a few drops of the remedy on the end of your tongue every time you feel you need to be rescued, and rescue you it will.

And finally...
Only the truly healthy
suffer a hangover—well done!

WHERE TO GET EVERYTHING

• • •

All supplements mentioned are available in pill form, tincture, or powder from all good health-food shops and some major supermarkets.

Try to check that no yeast, talcum, gelatines, etc., are included. You just want the pure stuff—nothing added and nothing taken away.

- **Essential oils** are very widely available from health-food stores and major pharmaceutical chains, like Whole Foods www.wholefoodsmarket.com. You can also order from the internet.
  - *Fragrant Earth* supply fabulous essential oils by mail order. www.fragrantearth.com
  - *Fleur Oils* do the same. www.fleur.co.uk
- **Oxygen** is available on the internet at www.OGOlife.com. Peppermint-scented pure oxygen in a 5-minute supply cannister should be enough to give you the boost you need.

- **Les Sources de Caudalie** are in Bordeaux in France. Browse their site on www.sources-caudalie.com. If you can't get to France, try locating a vinotherapie spa closer to you on www.spaindex.com/Lifestyles/VineyardSpas.htm.

INDEX

● ● ●

ABOUT THE AUTHOR

• • •

Jane Scrivner established the British School of Complementary Therapy in London's Harley Street in 1991. It offers full- and part-time courses in a range of therapies including therapeutic massage, reflexology, and aromatherapy.

Jane Scrivner lives in Stratford-upon-Avon and London. She is regularly featured in the media and her previous books include the bestselling *Detox Yourself*. Her website is www.janescrivner.com.